The Farewell Suites

The Poiema Poetry Series

Poems are windows into worlds; windows into beauty, goodness, and truth; windows into understandings that won't twist themselves into tidy dogmatic statements; windows into experiences. We can do more than merely peer into such windows; with a little effort we can fling open the casements, and leap over the sills into the heart of these worlds. We are also led into familiar places of hurt, confusion, and disappointment, but we arrive in the poet's company. Poetry is a partnership between poet and reader, seeking together to gain something of value—to get at something important.

Ephesians 2:10 says, "We are God's workmanship . . ." *poiema* in Greek— the thing that has been made, the masterpiece, the poem. The Poiema Poetry Series presents the work of gifted poets who take Christian faith seriously, and demonstrate in whose image we have been made through their creativity and craftsmanship.

These poets are recent participants in the ancient tradition of David, Asaph, Isaiah, and John the Revelator. The thread can be followed through the centuries—through the diverse poetic visions of Dante, Bernard of Clairvaux, Donne, Herbert, Milton, Hopkins, Eliot, R. S. Thomas, and Denise Levertov—down to the poet whose work is in your hand. With the selection of this volume you are entering this enduring tradition, and as a reader contributing to it.

—D.S. Martin
Series Editor

The Farewell Suites

ANDREW LANSDOWN

CASCADE *Books* · Eugene, Oregon

Other books by Andrew Lansdown

Poetry

Homecoming
Counterpoise
Windfalls
Waking and Always
The Grasshopper Heart
Between Glances
Abiding Things: Poems, stories, essays
Primary Loyalties (with Hal Colebatch and Peter Kocan)
Fontanelle
Birds in Mind: Australian nature poems
Far from Home: Poems of faith, grief and gladness
The Colour of Life (in *Two Poets* with Kevin Gillam)
Gestures of Love: The fatherhood poems
Inadvertent Things: Poems in traditional Japanese forms
Distillations of Different Lands
Abundance: New and Selected Poems
Little Studies in Loveliness
Filling the Emptiness

Poetry for Children

A Ball of Gold: Poems for children
Allsorts: Poetry tricks and treats

Poetry & Photography

Kyoto Sakura Tanka [Poems and photographs of Japan in spring]
Kyoto Momiji Tanka: Poems and photographs of Japan in autumn

Short Stories

The Bowgada Birds
The Dispossessed

Novels

With My Knife
Beyond the Open Door (USA edition of *With My Knife*)
Dragonfox
The Red Dragon
The Chronicles of Klarin

THE FAREWELL SUITES

Poiema Poetry Series

Cascade Books
An Imprint of Wipf and Stock Publishers
199 W. 8th Ave., Suite 3
Eugene, OR 97401

www.wipfandstock.com

PAPERBACK ISBN: 979-8-3852-2390-9
HARDCOVER ISBN: 979-8-3852-2391-6
EBOOK ISBN: 979-8-3852-2392-3

Cataloguing-in-Publication data:

Names: Lansdown, Andrew, author.

Title: The Farewell Suites / by Andrew Lansdown.

Description: Eugene, OR: Cascade Books, 2024 | Poiema Poetry Series | Includes bibliographical references and index.

Identifiers: ISBN 979-8-3852-2390-9 (paperback) | ISBN 979-8-3852-2391-6 (hardcover) | ISBN 979-8-3852-2392-3 (ebook)

Subjects: LCSH: Poetry. | Christian poetry.

Classification: CALL NUMBER 2024 (paperback) | CALL NUMBER (ebook)

VERSION NUMBER 08/05/24

For my wife, Susan

In memoriam
my father & mother, Colyn & Lois
my brothers, Stephen, Philip & David

'For we are strangers before thee, and sojourners, as were all our fathers: our days on the earth are as a shadow, and there is none abiding.'

—*THE HOLY BIBLE*, 1 CHRONICLES 29:15 (KJV)

Contents

V. For my mother

VI. For my third brother, the second attempt

VII. For my father

VIII. Coda

I

For my first brother
Stephen

1952–1973

Sounding-board

I remember, when my brother died,
placing my wristwatch facedown
on a literary journal in which a poem
of mine was published and hearing
quite unexpectedly in the pre-
dawn stillness the hollow sound
of its ticking, as if the magazine
cover had become a sounding-board
to amplify the tongue of time,
the silence between the seconds.

The Horseshoe Shooter

It is almost dark. A car passes
without its lights on. My son shoots it
with the hook end of his hockey stick.
'It shoots horseshoes,' he says.
I imagine a horseshoe
lobbing neatly onto the peg of the driver's neck.
'Piaow! Piaow!' cries my daughter,
improvising with her finger.
'Was this yours?' The old stick
is a new gift from his grandparents.
'No,' I say. 'It was my brother's.'
'Uncle David's?' My daughter is merely
revising the relationships: Dad's brother, my uncle.
'No. My brother Stephen. He's dead.'
They are both suddenly quiet. Their father
has a brother who is dead. Our father.
'Did you have any other brothers?'
'Yes. Philip.' 'Is he dead?' 'Yes.'
The horseshoe shooter has become a music stick
piping death from the basket of my life.
It rises up, the old snake, flicks
its forked tongue, flares its hood, sways, holds
them mesmerised. 'Were you grown up?'
They are thinking of each other now,
these little children, my son and daughter,
brother and sister. If Dad was a boy when . . .
are *we* safe? 'Yes,' I say.
Well, almost. 'Yes, I was grown up.'

They are relieved. But my daughter asks,
'And are you the oldest?'
'Well, I am now.' 'Good,' she says,
as if all uncertainties were now
settled, as if night were now the only darkness
coming upon the world. 'Good.'

Almost

'If I was standing
before God, I would still say
that there is no God,'
my brother said not long before
turning to God on his sickbed.

Almost as late as
the thief nailed beside the Lord
of Grief and Glory—
my brother repented and
pleaded to be remembered.

Knocking

I was eighteen
when my older brother died.
I barely cried, but
from that time on, if not before,
I've heard death knocking at my door.

II

For my second brother
Philip

1956–1978

Gone

'Gone!' our son puzzles
while looking for milk in an empty cup.

'Gone!' he says in amazement,
pointing to the light that has been switched off.

'Gone!' he urges, demanding my attention
as the record finishes and the music fades.

We usually laugh: one word
for so many occasions! 'Yes,' we say. 'Gone, gone.'

But today it is a burden to us
to be reminded all day long.

We are sealed off from joy,
seared by the news of your death.

Black Holes

Everywhere, death. In deep space
there are giant stars collapsed
into themselves, compressed
by their own weight.
As with a terrible grief,
their gravity is so great
not even light can escape.

It is hard to conceive:
black holes—voids
in the vacuum of space.

How long has it been
since the light left your face?
The heavens, my heart—
still I can't tell them apart.

For Philip

This is what death has done:
Changed him beyond belief
Made him blind and dumb

Turned him cold to the sun
Blown him away like a leaf:
This is what death has done.

 Can a tune beat time
 On the drum of his ear
 Now silence is the sound
 That alone draws near?

Seeing his form, we are numb:
For whom did we make this wreath?
He is blind and dumb.

We huddle together as one,
Yet each alone in our grief.
This is what death has done.

 Can a maiden dance
 In the chamber of his heart
 Now his blood is still
 And he's set apart?

My mother mourns her son,
But tears are cold relief:
He is blind and dumb.

The words that twist my tongue
Are bitter beyond all grief:
Look what death has done—
Made him blind and dumb!

Will the Day Star rise
To the circle of his sight?
Will his tongue peal praise
To the Father of Light?

I Do Not Forget

i

Sharing a dreadful purpose,
they arrived in the early morning—
my father and mother, my one remaining
brother—redeyed and riven with regret.

Philip is dead.

Death's ebony crook
hooked me
into the fold of grief.
Like sheep without a good shepherd
we huddled together.

ii

These days, when my father or mother
come to our home without warning,
I panic.

iii

He died while I slept.
Unknown to me, there was a moment
when the sweet and dreaming air
lapped into my lungs
but drained from his forever.
He died while I slept. Like a dream
he was gone when I awoke.

iv

Forever?

I believe
those who believe
share Christ's insurrection
against death.

Did he believe?

v
They wheeled the coffin
into the arctic room.

Like musk oxen,
we bunched together
to face the wolf of death.

vi
He lay dead in the coffin like a dead man.
Like a dead man he lay dead in the coffin.

vii
His right eyelid was slightly ajar
and death stared out at me
through the white of his eye.

viii
As we followed the heartblack hearse
I knew as never before:
Death is utterly perverse!

ix
At the graveside
I was appalled by apparitions
of decay.

x

After the funeral, we looked for photographs.

Like scavengers, my father and I
searched among his things
—picked through the flotsam
of his life, the debris
death had washed onto the shores of grief.

We found soiled snapshots
of his stereo, his dog—
but no picture of his face, nothing
to give relief.

We gave his stereo to the aimless
deathdazed youths
who shared his rented house.
I kept a photograph of the dog
leaping up at a hand
that might have been his.

At home, we rummaged
through drawers and albums—found him
strangely absent
from recent photographs of family
reunions and rituals—as if
our cameras had conspired with death
to efface even a record of his face.

xi

As Norsemen longed for ships
my brother pined for dogs.

I grieved for birds
and built cages. But our father
faltered at the prospect
of fluff on the carpet,
nip on the lawn. So Philip
was bereft of dogs
during his childhood days.

Long after the demon of his youth
had driven him from the family home
he was given a pup. It thrived
on his inarticulate love—
            and died
in the car smash that killed him.

The Viking went down with his ship.

      xii
I do not forget.

Grief

It is nothing tangible, no action, no word that has been said,
Just a feeling that sweeps the soul quite without warning
As a wind brushes the growing grain briefly on a calm morning.
It is a grief, a sudden remembrance that he is dead.

It is a feeling and a fact that God alone may understand.
Though I strain to remember, I long to forget.
But neither gives refuge or relief: either holds sorrow and regret.
He is gone: the cup is broken, the water spilt upon the sand.

Like a haunted theatre, there are lights and sounds in my head.
My mind flicks through old film, jams on an almost forgotten frame:
I see his face, hear his voice—and mine, whispering his name.
And for a moment there is nothing, no one I would rather instead.

It dies quickly, lies lightly like an autumn leaf.
But who knows what winds may flick it up again, this grief?

III

For our child

1992

In Memoriam

i

We knew something was wrong
because of the blood
but we had not expected this.
'I can't find a heartbeat,'
the doctor says. 'I'm sorry.'

ii

Dear child you died
in the secret safe place
alone. What did you suffer?
How could we have known?
Oh son, daughter, I'm sorry.

iii

I collected the images
from the ultrasound, the record,
child, of your short life
and long death. I burnt them
to spare your mother. I'm sorry.

Miscarriage

It's a miscarriage
whichever way you view it—
the ruin that reaves
an infant before breathing
and leaves a mother grieving.

If not in the womb,
then in the heart the unborn
grow big and bigger.
Oh, little mother, don't weep—
your child's now in Jesus' keep.

The Liminal Child

Now and then I yearn
for the child we lost, the one
without face or name,
who first leapt out of our love
and then leapt out of our lives.

It was hard on you,
child, but we also endured strife.
We couldn't conceive
that when we loved you into life
you'd enter our hearts like a knife.

Unsent Letters

i

Is all well with you?
I can't help but wonder, child,
what's become of you
since you went without a word
into Heaven's ward and ward.

ii

Maybe for you, child,
it was not a miscarriage . . .
Maybe it was good
you escaped to the New World
before being soiled or cruelled.

iii

Little one, in case
you're fretting about our hurt,
I'm writing to say:
We know, we know where you are
and soon, soon we'll join you there.

IV

For my third brother
the first attempt
David

1993

He Knows a Place

He knows a place we cannot share,
a wholly black and boundless space,
and when he went he drew us there.

It is the rift left in a tear,
a bullet or a blade's wet trace,
this place he knows we cannot share.

It is the darkness called despair
that none survive except by grace.
And when he went he drew us there.

Don't go, beloved! Oh, beware!
Don't turn your heart and set your face
upon that place we cannot share!

Sorrow and sickness were the fare
that gave him passage to that place.
And when he went he drew us there.

It barely counts how much we care.
This is the fact we must embrace:
he knows a place we cannot share,
and when he went he drew us there.

Waiting

i

Waiting and waiting
in the waiting room, we watch
each other waiting.

ii

In the waiting room
even the white carnations
are hanging their heads.

iii

In the end the nurse
comes to tell us we may wait
alongside his bed.

Intensive Care

Half conscious, for no
apparent reason, he counts
to five. We beam at
each other across his bed.
'What comes after five?'
my father asks this man who
is his son. We wait.
A doctor comes and goes. Then,
in a thin voice, 'Six.'
Who can tell from day to day
what will give us joy?
Barely four days since his head
injury—and already . . . !

Pathos

There is no bound to a father's
suffering and love. Ask our Father.

Ask mine. See how gently he is
tilting my brother's wounded head

to shave the stubble from his jaw.

V

For my mother
Lois

1930–2009

Mother

She is gone, the gap
of two deaths and two departures
cradled in her lap:

the old family album
with corners like thistles
and leaves clad in autumn.

'There you all are at Christmas
with your hats and whistles;
and that's you in the grass

with Teddy Lansdown. Remember?'

Family

'There's no one as good as us,
is there, Mum?' my grandmother said
my mother said when she was young.
So, without forethought or fuss,

she defined, as only children can,
her family and herself: familiar
with the lineaments of love, she felt
at home in her home. As a man

I hear her speak, this woman who
was once a girl my father never
knew. My mother, in all her grief
and grace. As if they were new

she remembers the old sureties
and shares them now with me—
this woman whom I love because
like Christ she first loved me.

Mother, oh, be assured of this:
what is true for you is true for me
(and may my children say the same),
'There's no one, not one as good as us!'

Prayer

Oh, for my mother in her pain,
Almighty and all-loving Lord,
I come to plead with you again.

For years her body's been a bane,
Putting all gladness to the sword:
Oh, for my mother in her pain!

Too much misery makes a stain
To black all light and block all laud:
I come to plead with you again.

Today at least relieve the strain
And give reprieve as a reward,
Oh, for my mother in her pain.

I know there is no other Name.
Despite the fact my faith is flawed,
I come to plead with you again.

Although my many sins maintain
That I deserve to be ignored—
Oh, for my mother in her pain
I come to plead with you again!

Fellowship

My mother called it
'The Fellowship of the Back',
this misery we shared,
this pain in our spines that spoilt
all our joys, with nothing spared.

The Last Entry

Ten days before she died
my mother wrote, 'Colyn
cut my toenails today.'

And with this last entry
in her notepad diary
she perfectly expressed

the contraction of the life
and the expansion of the love
she shared with my father.

Prank Call

In my dream I breathed heavily
into the telephone mouthpiece.

I was wanting to make a sound,
send a sensation, of menace

down the pathways of wire and air
to set the caller's heart quailing.

I breathed heavily in my dream,
lacing each lung-gust with a growl,

until I was stopped, mortified,
by a voice wheezy with asthma

and love, a voice saying my name.
And in my dream I woke and said,

'Oh Mother, Mother, forgive me!'
But she never did, being dead.

Dearly Departed

So much of it, my childhood,
departed this world with you.

Though I lived it, I can bring back
only brief moments of it:

candle-smoke and a blue trike,
a Band-Aid on a skinned knee,

your comforting hugs during
nights of dread dreams about . . . what?

Mother, I meant to ask you
so many things about me,

so many whens, hows and whys
that can never now be known.

The loss of both your presence
and my history presses on me

as an ever-present absence.

Evocations

Unlikeliest things
can ignite or inflame grief . . .
Today the bamboo's
swollen knuckles remind me
of my dead mother's dear hands.

Sacred Harp Singers

I am watching *Awake, My Soul*, my first watching,
first hearing, first introduction to the astonishing
shape-note singing of the Sacred Harp songs,
the white spirituals of the American deep south—

sacred hymns for the sacred harp set in the human
throat, that twin-cord multi-chord lyre lodged
in every locket-adorned or V-lumped neck,
the image-bearer's instrument, the instrument

the soul can play to sound out its praise and passion
for the Good Shepherd and Guardian of our Souls—
and listening my soul awakes to the utter completion
and negation of self as together each singer hurtles out

the sharp shape-notes of the chosen canto—
and the company of these unaccompanied voices
rouses the rivalry, I imagine, of cherubim and archangels
who join in competition and communion to raise

another *a cappella* anthem of praise and elation,
and with their contrapuntal halleluing and hullaballooing
the duet choirs dare to charm, dare even to daze
our common Creator, our matchless Maker, the Almighty—

and transported of a sudden I am thinking
of my mother, my mother who has gone
into the presence of our Saviour, my mother,
who left me half-orphaned half a year ago—

and I am wishing I could share this discovery,
this delirious delight with her, could say to her,
'Mother dear, Mum, listen, look'—and the raw
rollicking raucous singing would lift her, thrill her,

as would, even more, the words, the mighty majestic
meanings of these Earth-birthed Heaven-homing hymns
flowing from the sad keen glad hearts of singers,
sinners in love with the lovely Lord who loves us

and gave himself for us, the Lion of Judah,
the Lamb of God, the Once and Future King
whose sword and salve will swathe and save the world—
but she is not here, my mother, not here

to hear this great grand noise of a hundred
human voices hollering into the holy ear
of the Most High, and I am startled by a sense
of loss, loneliness, longing, torn by a sudden

sadness for myself and my motherlessness,
grieved regardless of the realisation that she is likely
right now listening to all the glory-gathered larynx-lyred
singers boxed about the Throne, listening enthralled

as they yell out their discordant harmonies—
until mid-word, mid-note they are stopped,
hushed by the surprising regal rising of his Majesty,
who peers past the foursquare ranks of the chanters,

past the first blessed billion behind them,
and motions to my mother, my mother,
shorter than Zacchaeus and short of a sycamore,
and he says to her, my mother, my father's darling,

our Father's daughter, 'Lois,' he says, using the name
we know her by, her username, not the new name,
the white-stone name, the secret sobriquet
of immeasurable intimacy he gave her when

he guided her through the Valley of the Shadow—
'Lois,' he beckons, 'Come closer, closer in,'
and she blushes and curtsies and makes her way
through the multitude, through the Red-Sea-parting

throng to the Throne, and he says, 'Sit here,
here with the sopranos,' and she smiles the shy-sure
smile of one who is loved, and unconsciously
the angels smooth their robes as she smooths

her dress to sit, and he says, 'Tune your harp,
little sister, tune your harp and sing!'

VI

For my third brother
the second attempt
David

1961–2012

Missing

The last time I wrote to my last brother
I lacked the words, so I wrote the words
of The Innocence Mission—wrote them as I recalled them,
enhanced by the singer's melody and phrasing:

> *And I can only say*
> *that I had hoped for you*
> *safety from fears and darkness.*
> *Are you feeling better than before?*

I got up from the tossing bed
where the thoughts of him missing
and the feelings of missing him
would not let go my heart or leave my head
and I wrote, *And I can only say . . .*
and I sent these words into cyberspace
in the frail hope they might find him
and in finding impart a form of grace.

But I could not send them singing
and I could not send them straight—
and besides it was far, far too late.
In the innocence of despair he was on a mission
to decimate despair—and how was I to know
he had accomplished it already?

Oh, save for doubts, I am all unsteady—
yet truly, brother, beyond all saying

I can only say
that I had hoped for you
safety from fears and darkness!

I am sorry, sorry I did not send these words to you before,
before you were feeling poorer than before.

And now I can only say: Since you have gone to stay
with the sweet Man of Sorrows who is acquainted
with all your grief, I am glad you must be feeling better,
better, little brother, than even your best before.
But how can I find safety from the fears and darkness,
the tears and starkness, you abandoned at my door?

Variations of Sorrow

i
Running

Brother, you ran, ran,
ran like the Gingerbread Man
fast and far from us:
you ran and you ran and then
you never came back again.

ii
Cutting

As a cutter cuts
a human shape out of raw
gingerbread dough—
so death, brother, cut the stark
shape of you out of my heart.

iii
Flattening

Forgive me, brother,
but I must try to forget—
for thinking of you
flattens me and spreads me thin,
like dough beneath a rolling pin.

Forgetting

'I long to pick/ Some forgetting-grass'—
Ki no Tsurayuki, The Tosa Diary, 935 AD

For you I need a different flower,
brother, than the blue forget-me-nots.

Here, here in this world where you left me
I yearn for the sweet forgetting-grass

treasured by the ancient Japanese.
I want to search out and gather up

those grasses that take away grieving
by somehow infusing forgetting.

I want stooks of the stuff, large wigwam
stooks that can be shaken loose and strewn

to cover me with stalk, leaf and scent
from the loss of you and how you went.

The Sure and Certain Hope

Do not think of it,
the state of his body
after weeks in the car
in the remote ranges
in the summer heat.

Think rather of the fact
that before the fumes
filled the cabin and his lungs
he wrote an apology
to his wife and children

and read (according to
the Bible he left
opened on the dash)
Mary's Magnificat
for his final devotion.

VII

For My Father
Colyn

1926–2022

The Grandsons

for Stephen, Jesse, Seth & Ashley

My four sons—
three from my wife's body,
the fourth from my daughter's wedding—

my four boys—
how lovely they were
to my father, their grandfather,

when he fell
to the kitchen floor
and through it into feebleness.

My wife and I
were, when he fell,
holidaying half a continent away

and our four sons
tended him tenderly,
tag-teaming the days and nights until

we returned
to take over the task
of feeding, bathing and bedding him.

Our four sons—
for kindness and care,
who in this world can compare?

The Tombstone Trail

The start of his fail was his fall.
Down he went, walking-stick and all.

It gave him bruises, but not brakes.
And yet, a tumble's all it takes

to exhaust the elderly's strength
and reduce autonomy's length.

We moved in to take care of him
half-hoping he'd regain his vim.

But his fall was the start of his fail,
his first step on the Tombstone Trail.

The Goodnight Rite

After I have tucked him in,
drawn the coverlet up to his chin,
I kneel to kiss his forehead
and rub his shoulder. Usually,
he thanks me, my nonagenarian father,
smiling toothlessly from his pillow.

Then, as is the ritual, I switch off
the electric under-blanket,
and I answer, 'Yes, at the wall, too.'
And I accept the legitimacy:
for he worries since that time
I forgot and he woke in a swelter,
a claustrophobia of heat,
and had to claw himself out,
out into the spacious cold.

Lastly, before leaving him
to his diminishing dreams,
I do a final reconnoitre . . .
Yes, his slippers are facing
the way he likes. His shirt and pants
are folded and placed as preferred.
His hearing aid, its battery ejected,
is on a clean tissue on the dresser.
His flashlight and his phone
are set nearby in the white space
once filled by another pillow.
And his wheeled walking-frame is stationed
one step short of the bed-end,
its handbrake on so that when
he startles it with his grip in the morning
it will not giddy-up before he is ready.

And as I flick the light switch
by the door, he instructs me
as usual and as usual I reply,
'No, I won't close it.' And I don't.
I simply step into the passage,
wondering if tomorrow night,
before the darkness pulls its shroud
over his head, I might get
yet one more chance to draw
the coverlet up to his chin,
tug it up and tuck it tightly in,
as he did for me in my infancy,
wanting only my welfare,
only my good in time and eternity.

Watching

I am watching, watching my father
walking . . . It catches me by surprise

to see him totter into open space
where no handhold can steady or save him.

He is like a man traversing a tightrope
for the first time—and the last, should he fall.

He is so absorbed in the exercise
he does not notice my absorption.

I am taut as a rope stretched to breaking—
any moment I might whip out to catch him.

And all the while I am watching him,
his walking-frame stands nearby, aghast.

Hailing Help

I settle my father in his bed
then retire to mine. I leave
the doors to our rooms ajar
in case he calls for help in the night.

And tonight, in the blackest
hours of morning, he does.
I am reached and roused
by the sound of his voice.

I rise and enter the passage
then pause, uncertain of what
I am hearing. It is him alright.
But what is he saying, wanting?

I lean into the dark, listening.
No, he is not voicing distress
but devotion—not hailing help
but praising Heaven.

There is no doubting it—
that thin sound in the thick night.
He is singing, singing a hymn,
a homage-song to his Redeemer.

It wrenches me into wretchedness,
arrests all my attention and emotion—
the weakness of his warble,
the unexpectedness of his worship.

My brave and steadfast father—
he sounds so small and lonely
singing songs of deliverance
in the near-dawn darkness.

How long has he been awake,
how long singing, singing
in the big bed he has shared
for years with no companion?

I linger, listening. It seems
I am not required . . . and yet
I am not released. I cannot
return to my bed, my sleep.

Angels elbow me for a place
at his doorway, jostle me until
Jesus arrives with an appalling
look of compassion on his face.

A Roundabout Report

He has a habit of circumlocution,
but who can blame him on this occasion?

Not long lodged in the aged-care home,
he's adjusting to life in a single room.

Earlier this week, he shared a repast
with a fellow inmate and spoke of Christ.

It was his first venture past the nurses
into company and cutlery noises.

And now with customary recapitulations
and somewhat more than usual hesitations

and an at-first (forgive me) frustrating dearth
of directness, he tells me his possible friend

impossibly last night 'departed this earth'.

Aged Care

Returning from holiday,
we fetched my father
from the nursing home

and were shocked to see
a cream-coloured chrysanthemum
blooming in one eye—

a flower with petals of pus
his carers watched grow
without telling doctors or us.

The specialist we took him to
raged, 'How has his eye
been allowed to get in this state!'

And with his furious referral
we rushed my father to hospital
never guessing we were too late.

Dependency

Mashed potato—
not the hospital's
but my wife's,
with extra butter and salt.

'And gravy, too,' I say.
He half-opens his mouth.

I get in half a teaspoonful
before he clamps his lips
and turns his head—
the only actions of refusal
left to him.

He savours it for a moment,
then, with difficulty, swallows.

'Tasty, eh?' I say.

He turns his face
back towards my voice
and opens his mouth again,
opens it wide.

I recall from childhood
hungry canary hatchlings,
blind, bald, beaks agape,
pathetic in their perfect
dependency.

This seeing the sick,
a poet-priest once wrote,
endears them to us.

Yes, truly, he has never been
dearer to me, my father,
achingly dearer, than now.

Touching

How long can his body go on
with so little going in? And now
there is nothing coming out.

This morning, the nurse tells me,
they inserted a catheter
to drain his bladder. I shudder
as I settle in the chair by his bed.

My eyes keep returning to the tube
attaching him to the drainage bag,
a clear pliable plastic tube
with yellow liquid and air bubbles.

It is like, I think, the connecting tube
for an aquarium pump-and-filter.
It is like, I think, the final milestone
before the gravestone.

'Andrew,' he says, as if wanting
to share a confidence. 'Andrew.'
I lean closer. 'A woman
has been touching my penis.'

Dreadful, this delirium—letting him
perceive facts but not process them,
turning the true into the not-true.

In his perplexity and helplessness,
what violation did he feel,
this man of decency and fidelity,
my most-modest, monogamous father?
There is no measure for it,
the revulsion of the ravished.

'A woman has been touching . . . '

I try to explain about nurses
and catheters. He remains silent,
considering my comments . . .
and perhaps even believing them.

The Conspiracy

I am bending over his bed,
my face next to his, speaking
into his ear, into the hearing aid
with the new battery.

He is so sure of it, it is hard
to convince him otherwise.
But at last, I think he accepts
the doctors and nurses
are not scheming to kill him.

I stretch my back, sit down
and ponder what next to say.
Nothing seems relevant anymore.

Between long silences,
I tell him snippets of news—
my wife joining in, helping out,
as always. He listens, drifts
and sometimes responds.

A nurse comes to make us go.
Visiting time is long over.
We stand up in obedience
and begin our farewells.

As I bend to kiss his forehead,
he says conspiratorially
in strange gangster slang,
'I was supposed to have been
bumped off yesterday.'

It would be funny to us
were it not so frightful to him.

The Buzz

It lurches into buzz,
his electric shaver,

and I wonder if the noise
will be too loud

for his hearing aids
or perhaps add more din

to his dogged delirium.
Nonetheless, I begin.

We work as a team
to mow the stubble:

I manoeuvre the cutting
steel over his skin:

He stretches his neck,
juts his chin,

plumps his lips,
turns the other cheek.

Muzzling the buzz,
I ask, 'How's that?'

With draining effort,
he lifts his hand . . .

'A bit more here,'
he says. 'And here.'

I begin again, glad
to prolong the intimacy.

When at last he
is satisfied, I say,

'Now you look almost
as handsome as me.'

Quick as a whip he quips,
'Perish the thought!'

I am too surprised,
too delighted to retort.

Singing

Whether by fluke or by flash,
I break the slow silence
by his sickbed with a song—

a hymn I hope might make his heart
hum in the confounded place
to which age and ailment abducted him.

And, amazing beyond measure,
hardly have I begun before
he joins in—singing

all the words, in tune and in time.
Look—almost his head is lifting
from its pock in the pillow!

Listen—almost his voice is loud
from his food-refusing throat!
It is an astonishment absolute!

My father, oh my father—
helpless but not songless
in the last days of his desperation.

Then, jolting my joy, jeering,
a thought comes to me mid-song
that this is the last, the last

of anything we will ever do together.
And I am struck by the grief of it—
the galling, bawling grief!

But my voice goes on, dragging
my heart along . . . until . . .
until I sense this is also the best,

the choicest of everything
we have done as father and son—
this singing in unity and unison,

singing an anthem of the Kingdom,
a canticle for Heaven's Crown Prince.
And as we finish our duet,

I perceive a better truth yet,
and I think, Oh, it's just like him,
the Father's darling Dauphin,

the faithful's daring Deliverer—
it's just like him, isn't it?—to cast
the very best to us at the very last!

Don't Worry

'It's alright,' I say. The orderlies
are wheeling his bed into the corridor.

'They're just taking you to another ward.'
I don't say, the one for palliative care.

He turns his head and reaches towards
the sound of me. 'But how will I find you?'

Everything about him gives me grief,
my father, gripped by frailties and fears.

'Don't worry,' I say, 'I'll find *you*.'
And a little later for a little longer, I do.

Falling

'Hold me, Andrew!
Hold me tight!'
And I do.

I hug him hard,
half-lifting him
from his hospital bed.

My father. Delirium
has delivered him
to yet another dread.

This time, he tells me,
he is falling down,
down into darkness.

'It's alright,' I say.
'I've got you,' I say.
'You're not falling.'

But he is, he is
falling—falling
into a fathomless pit.

And it isn't my arms
he needs to feel
but those of the One

waiting to catch him.

The Temples

'Not one stone
will be left standing,'
Jesus said of the temple
in Jerusalem.

'Destroy this temple
and in three days
I will raise it up,'
he said of his own body.

'It is the temple
of the Holy Spirit,'
his apostle said
of the believer's body.

I think of these truths
in hospital as I gaze
down on my father—
my father, whose temple

lies in ruins, not one
stone on top of another.

Breaking Through

Not knowing what else to do,
searching for a way to break through

his exhaustion and delirium,
I begin to sing him a hymn.

I am so glad that our Father in Heaven
tells of his love in the book he has given . . .

And to our astonishment
he breaks out in accompaniment,

his neck straining from the pillow,
his throat issuing a frail bellow.

Wonderful things in the Bible I see,
this is the dearest that Jesus loves me . . .

Yes, this is the dearest, my dear.
Go on your way now without fear.

Shaving

Shaving again my dad
in the hospital bed

I recall how he shaved
a son who was not dead

even though he had fired
a bullet through his head.

Psalm of Importunity

He is in the holding paddock now,
this old ram who fathered me.
He is in want.

His right eye is blinded,
his left is darkly clouded.
He cannot see to walk
in the paths of righteousness.

And could he see,
he still could not walk.
He cannot stand even
or prop himself up.
He is made to lie down
in desolate places.

He will not eat
and we no longer coax him.
He cannot eat.
The tenderest of green grasses
grate on his gums
and ball in the back of his throat.

The anointing oil is rancid
in the thin wool of his head.
He is beyond healing.

His mind keeps wandering
into dark places.
Debilitations and dreads besiege him
in the presence of his friends.

Delirium tricks and taunts him:
You will fear all evil!
There are serpents in the pastures,
jackals in the sheepfold.
Wolves howl by the still waters.

Good Shepherd, won't you come,
come quickly
and carry him on your shoulders
through the Valley of the Shadow?

Comfort, comfort him
with your rod and your staff
and bear him to the meadowlands
where lambs frolic with lions
and saints and seraphim stroll.

For your name's sake,
renew his body, restore his soul.

The Betrayal

Black as the retina the surgeon removed—
that's how black his vision is
in what was his good eye. His other eye,
the uninfected one, has long been near-sightless.
Yet in his enfeebled state he seems somehow
not to have noticed his blindness.

Now, five weeks since the darkness took him,
he asks for his glasses, the ones
the optometrist prescribed just months ago.

Minutes ago, he asked me again
to take him out, out of the hospital,
and again I tried to explain why I can't.

Now, for the first time in all the time
he's been here, he asks me for his glasses.
Dear Lord, it's as if he'd dropped a boulder
on the barely-buoyant raft of my heart!
His glasses of all things! 'But Dad,'
I say, going under, sinking down, 'I don't
have them. They're at home. I'm sorry.'

And so is he . . . sorry beyond sorrow.

Instantly, impossibly, he slumps
deeper into his deathbed. It's as if, as if
my words were scissors and had snipped
the last of his sinews, turning the little tautness
left in his body into a terrible slackness.

More appalling still, and more impossibly too,
his emaciated face crumples, as if it were
a blown-up ball the scissors had punctured.

It is hopeless. Suddenly he sees it plainly.
Hopeless. His own son, his sole next-of-kin,
goaded by some incomprehensible unkindness,
has denied him even his glasses.

I look at the look on his face and look away.
It is a disappointment so deep
it is indistinguishable from despair.
It is the bruise betrayal leaves on the Belovèd's face.
It is, I imagine, like the look Jesus had
when during his trial he wrenched with a glance
such bitter weeping from Peter.

And yet . . . and yet . . . I reflect . . .
Peter at least had the consolation
of knowing Jesus was not mistaken.

Lamplight

The lamp of the Lord—
that's how the word of the Lord
describes the spirit of a man.

And looking at my father
sunken into his deathbed
I sense and see the truth of it.

Now his spirit has returned
(a little ruined, a lot redeemed)
to the Lord who gave it,

how dark it is, his body,
how utterly given over
to bleakness and blackness,

its lamplight all extinguished.

The Surprise

He did not know he was dying, my father.
Dreams and deliriums diverted his thoughts
in the final weeks of his fatal weakness.

Repeated times I told him the truth of it—
the bare brutal (and for him, a believer) blessed truth:
'You are going to see Jesus soon. Very soon,
Dad, you are going to see him face to face.'

But although I had replaced the batteries
in his hearing aid, he did not hear:

He asked for his walker, as if he could still walk.
He asked for his glasses, as if he could still see.
He asked for his torch, as if he could still switch it on,
as if he needed its light in the never-dark ward . . .

And he tore, tore at my heart:
'Andrew, take me out! Just take me out!'
As if . . . as if I could if only I would.

My father did not know he was dying,
could not comprehend the closing phase
of his earthly days had come.

So what an astonishment it must have been,
what a shock of amazement, when,
leaving his mortal remains in the hospital bed,
he entered the presence of the Belovèd,

the Belovèd and all his beloved.

Could Have Been

Had I not soon afterwards written them down,
our few words that day in the last of his wards,
I would nonetheless have remembered them
with clarity, as in fact I remember them now:

'You have been a good father to me,' I said,
my hand slipped under his pillowed head,
my forehead pressed against his. He was about
to depart this life downright against his will
and I wanted him to go with the assurance
of my love. 'You have been a good father . . . '

He was quiet, as he had been mostly in the weeks
since his admission, and I did not expect
a response. I hoped only that he had heard me
and that, hearing, he had understood
and that, understanding, he had been heartened,
his load lightened a little for the last distance.
Then, long after the moment had passed,
he responded, 'I could have been a better father.'

This was not what I expected, not at all
what I wanted—this tacit acknowledgement
of the hurts he dealt out to me in recent years,
the years of imbalance since half of him—
his wife, my mother—was lost to this world.
Can a weight-scale's pivot-beam remain level
when one end has lost its dangling dish?
It crashed down on me, his end of the beam,
and every effort to lift it seemed only
to bring it down on me again with more force.

'I could have been a better father,' he said.
And I could have agreed, aggrieved. But
it was comfort, not condemnation, I intended.
Besides, is it not a fact that for most of my life
he was, he truly was a good and loving father?
Should, as in Joseph's dream, the many fat years
be eaten up by the few lean? And anyway,
had not things been better between us at the last?

To consoled him and to quell any qualms, I said,
'I could have been a better son.' I *could* have been . . .
Let this be the end of it, I thought by his dying bed.
Let us clear by confession our charge sheet
so Christ on this count need not hold us to account
come the Day of Judgment. 'I could have been
a better son,' I said. 'So let's forgive each other.'

A few days later, he left the hospital for Heaven,
slipped away when I wasn't looking
even though I had been looking all night long.
He absconded to that place where repentance
is completed and remorse is defeated, that place
where forgiveness is never rescinded or repeated.

He has gone there and left me here,
here where none of those things are full or final—
here where the heart's wounds keep on weeping
and require swabbing and stitching seventy times seven—
here where the guilt of wrongs committed
and the shame of rights omitted never quite quit
troubling the soul in times of quietness—
here in this world where *could-have-beens*
are black clouds that can make the bluest skies wet
and replenish periodically the reservoir of regret.

The Sad News

It went on a while,
texts and calls to his cell phone.
Each time it was yet
one more person who was dazed
to learn his life has been razed.

Two Cities

He is now a denizen
of the City of the Dead

my father, my father
whose boxed body

we lowered to rest
atop my mother's—

the two of them
in the one tenement

of this necropolis,
this stopover city

on the long journey
to the City of God,

the city of which
glorious things are spoken.

That Space

It was always
a foreboding—that space
on the headstone
below my mother's name
now filled with my father's.

Those Stones

Set around the small fishless
but papyrus-sprouting pond,
four roughly-flat foot-sized stones
taken from my father's backyard
before his house was sold.

They have settled in place,
those stones, as if they always
belonged to me, as if they never
once belonged to another man
or took the weight of his tread.

Already the native violets
have cozied up to them,
resting their small green hands
on their rough-edged shoulders
as if they were long-time pals.

The lovely lush poolside violas . . .
Several even are waving
petite white-and-mauve pennants,
doing all in their power
to make them feel at home—

those stones, those stones
that once felt my father's footfall.

Struggling On

The native plant
that almost gave up after
I transplanted it
from my father's garden has
broken out in mauve florets.

These Papers

All these papers he put his life into—
sermon manuscripts and lecture outlines,
Bible study notes and children's talks,
meeting minutes and diary entries . . .
No one wants them, all these papers,
not even his last living son. For

what can I do with them all? When
would I ever get time even to read them?
I have mounds of my own writings—
essays and sermons, poems and stories—
to deal with, and more on the way,
more with more things I want to say.

I know, with something of the feeling
of my father's feeling, that come my time
to leave my home for a 'home',
my children, too, without malice
and maybe with a little sadness,
will likely compost the leaves of my life.

Instead of working at these writings,
I sometimes think I might as well
have grubbed the soft fern shoots
to stave my hunger, like the bowmen of Shu.
Sometimes like them I wonder
who can know our sorrow, who?

The Refreshening

It is surprising
how it refreshes the loss
every time I must
explain again that his soul
left his body in the dust.

The Book

When I was a boy, my father
showed me the beauty of the Book,
and its words were like the spit
Jesus spat in a blind man's eyes.

At first, I saw uncanny things—
people milling like trees walking.
Then I saw clearly—folk feasting
on the fruit of the Tree of Life.

It's before me now, the best of
my father's bequests, his Bible—
eight hundred sheets of rice paper
bound together in black leather.

But strangely, opposite the spine
at the top right corner, the book
is plainly plumped up, the pages
seemingly fattened or loosened there—

as if something microscopic
had permeated the paper to swell
at its unbound upper corner
the volume of the volume.

Flipping the pages, each as thin
as a nonagenarian's skin,
I note the corners are crinkled,
like the skim on simmering milk.

And I realise this spot is where
he fumbled to turn the pages,
first dabbing forefinger to tongue
to moisten it to get a grip.

And I wince at the thought of it
until I sense our good Sovereign
has infused these holy pages
with salve from his devout servant

to brighten from their blindness
the eyes, the peepers, of my soul.

Finalities

I removed his name
from my address book today,
my deceased father.
Tonight, I found it once more
among my email contacts.

My Father and Our Queen

i.m. Colyn L & Elizabeth R

He was born the same year as the Queen,
and died the same year, this year, too.

Like her, except with a fortnight's start,
my father passed from hope to certainty.

Like her, only not as a ruler but
as a pastor, he was faithful to his calling.

Last week, two hundred paused for his funeral.
This week, two billion for the Queen's.

She rightly will be remembered by nations,
he only by grandchildren, churches and friends.

And yet, I think His Majesty in eternity
will give him also an amaranthine coronet.

Apart from Blood

I do not know when I first knew
I loved you, but from my youth
I have loved you more and more.

And while, apart from blood,
there are reasons,
surely one is to the fore:

Your life has spoken
the mysterious grammar of godliness,
the deep logic of love and law.

Father, if in eternity I have a place,
it is because (no matter how jaded)
I first saw Jesus in your face.

VIII

Coda

Night Petals, Shirakawa Canal

Gion, Kyoto, Japan

An oblong of light
laid on the canal surface
from a café window—
and sometimes cherry petals
drifting through from dark to dark . . .

Lovely but lonely
to see them passing by on
the canal's surface—
petals with their pale faces
like those of the ones we love.

Sakura Haiku

with Susan in Kyoto in spring

The falling petals—
almost they make us forget
we are immortals.

Notes

Sacred Harp Singers

Awake, My Soul is a film about Sacred Harp (shape-note) singing practiced for over 200 years by some church congregations in the American south. It was released on DVD in 2007 by Awake Productions, Atlanta.

Missing

Lyrics quoted from the song 'You Are the Light' by The Innocence Mission on the album *Birds of My Neighbourhood* (Badman Recording Co., 2006)

Dependency

Lines quoted from the poem 'Felix Randal' by Gerard Manley Hopkins.

The Temples

Matthew 24:2; John 2:19; 1 Corinthians 6:19.

Breaking Through

Lyrics quoted from the hymn 'Jesus Loves Even Me' by Emily S. Oakey and Philip P. Bliss.

Lamplight

Proverbs 20:27.

These Papers

References 'The Song of the Bowmen of Shu' by Li Po, translated from the Chinese by Ezra Pound.

Acknowledgements

Poems in this collection have appeared in the following publications: *Love: 2023 ACU Prize for Poetry Anthology*; *Antipodes* (U.S.A.); *Cuttlefish: Western Australian Poets*; *Eucalypt: A Tanka Journal*; *inScribe: 2022 Grieve Anthology*; *Poetry d'Amour 2023*; *Practical Theology* (U.K.); *Quadrant*; *Seagift*; *Studio*; *The Weekend Australian*; and *Westerly*.

Some of the poems in this collection (occasionally with minor revisions) have been taken from some of the poet's other books. Details of these books can be found on his website at www.andrewlansdown.com.

'A Roundabout Report' was first published in *Practical Theology* (Volume 15, Issue 3, 2022), available online at: www.tandfonline.com/doi/full/10.10 80/1756073X.2022.2047249.

The Poiema Poetry Series

The Book of Bearings by Diane Glancy
In a Strange Land anthology edited by D.S. Martin
What I Have I Offer With Two Hands by Jacob Stratman
Slender Warble by Susan Cowger
Madonna, Complex by Jen Stewart Fueston
No Reason by Jack Stewart
Abundance by Andrew Lansdown
Angelicus by D.S. Martin
Trespassing on the Mount of Olives by Brad Davis
The Angel of Absolute Zero by Marjorie Stelmach
Duress by Karen An-hwei Lee
Wolf Intervals by Graham Hillard
To Heaven's Rim anthology edited by Burl Horniachek
Cup My Days Like Water by Abigail Carroll
Soon Done with the Crosses by Claude Wilkinson
House of 49 Doors by Laurie Klein
Hawk and Songbird by Susan Cowger
Ponds by J. C. Scharl

www.ingramcontent.com/pod-product-compliance
Lightning Source LLC
Chambersburg PA
CBHW022033090426

42741CB00007B/1053